Filipino Cookbook

*Traditional Filipino Recipes
Made Easy*

www.grizzlypublishing.com

Table of Contents

Introduction

I want to thank you for purchasing this book, *'Filipino Cookbook: Traditional Filipino Recipes Made Easy.'*

There are more than seven thousand islands, with varied cultures and geographies that comprise the Philippines. Filipino cuisine is simple, tropical and consists of various native dishes that suit the varied geography of the region. The main ingredients of traditional Filipino cuisine consist of seafood, chicken, pork, citrusy fruits, tomatoes, garlic and onions. Also, rice is the staple starch of this region, like any other country in South Asia.

Over time, the influence of different regions has shaped Filipino cuisine. Filipino food is a beautiful blend of Chinese, Malay and other South-Asian cuisine. Signature ingredients of any Southeast Asian food include coconuts, pungent fish sauces, chilies and lime. You will find all these and other flavorful ingredients in Filipino recipes.

Perhaps, Filipino food is the least well-known of all Southeast Asian cuisine in the world. It features a strong influence of Spanish, Chinese and American cultures and cuisine. What it lacks for is a singular national identity that is the defining trait for cuisine in other regions, but it makes up for this with amazing flavors. It is not easy to define Filipino food and, perhaps, it is this indefinability that makes Filipino food interesting and quite tasty.

From delicious snacks to delectable seafood recipes and tasty rice and noodle dishes, this book is truly a delight! Filipino fare will make you fall in love with food all over again.

If you are looking for a cookbook that features a wide array of recipes that showcases different flavors, textures and ingredients, then this is the best book for you. The recipes curated in this book include tasty appetizers, entrees and desserts. The recipes mentioned in this book will certainly tingle your taste buds and will leave you wanting more. The recipes are quite easy to understand and simple to follow. If you follow these simple recipes, you will be able to cook delicious Filipino dishes within no time. The one thing that you need to do is gather all the necessary ingredients and start cooking. Trying different recipes is the best way to learn about the cuisine of any region and the same stands true for Filipino cooking as well.

So, if you are ready to learn more about traditional Filipino cuisine, then let us start without further ado.

Since the 11th century, Chinese traders were involved in trade with the Philippines. It wasn't just silk and ceramics that they brought with them. Along with all this, they introduced different ingredients and cooking techniques as well. The common Chinese cooking methods like stir-frying and steaming are commonly used in Filipino cuisine. The famous Filipino pancit is quite similar to the noodle soup dishes that are popular in China, lumpia is similar to Chinese spring rolls and siaomai is quite similar to Chinese dim sums. Therefore, it is safe to say that Filipino cuisine has taken a strong influence from Chinese cuisine.

During the 16th century, the Philippines was colonized by Spaniards. Spaniards exposed Filipinos to Catholicism along with olive oil, paprika, saffron, cheese and cured sausages. In fact, Spanish paella is a great example of how Spanish cuisine wove its way into the heart of Philippines. During late 1800s, the Philippines was colonized by the United States. The Americans introduced Filipinos to different techniques or convenient cooking techniques like pressure-cooking, pre-cooking, salads and fried chicken and much more. The Filipino culture managed to adapt these foreign recipes and cooking methods and tweaked them to suit the native needs.

Chapter One: Filipino Breakfast Recipes

Longsilog (Sausage with Garlic Rice and Fried Egg)

Serves: 4

Ingredients:

- 8 pieces longanisa (sausage)
- 4 eggs
- Salt to taste
- 2-4 tablespoons minced garlic
- 2 tablespoons oil
- 4 cups chilled white rice
- 2 cups water

Method:

1. To make longanisa: Place a pan over medium heat. Pour water into the pan.
2. Add sausage and bring to a boil. Let it boil until dry. Turn the sausage a couple of times.
3. When dry, let the sausage fry. Turn the sausage a couple of times until they are cooked well on all the sides and crisp outside. Turn off the heat.
4. To make garlic fried rice: Place a pan over medium heat. Add oil. When the oil is heated, add garlic and sauté until brown.
5. Add rice. Stir-fry for a few minutes. Add salt and stir for a few more minutes. Turn off the heat.
6. Cook the eggs, sunny side up.
7. Serve 2 longanisa in each plate with an egg and 1-cup garlic fried rice.

Note: This garlic-fried rice is a side dish and can be used in many main course recipes.

Pork Tocino (Sweet Cured Pork)

Serves: 6-7

Ingredients:

- 3 pounds pork, thinly sliced
- 1/3 cup lemon-lime soda
- 1/3 cup soy sauce
- Oil, as required
- Red food coloring, a few drops (optional)
- 1 cup + 2 tablespoons brown sugar
- 1/3 cup pineapple juice
- ¾ teaspoon garlic powder
- 3 cups water

To serve:

- Garlic fried rice – refer previous recipe
- Fried eggs

Method:

1. Add sugar, garlic powder, lemon-lime soda and garlic powder into an airtight container. Stir until sugar dissolves completely.
2. Add pork and toss until pork is well coated. Close the lid and chill in the refrigerator for curing. Keep it for 1-3 days.
3. To cook: Place a large pan over medium high heat. Add water and pork along with the cured mixture.
4. Simmer until dry. Add a little oil and cook until light brown on the edges of the pork. Turn off the heat.
5. Serve with garlic fried rice and fried eggs.

Champorado (Chocolate Rice Porridge)

Serves: 8

Ingredients:

- 1 ½ cups glutinous rice, rinsed in water a couple of times until it runs clear
- ¾ cup brown sugar
- Evaporated milk or condensed milk, as required
- 6 tablespoons cocoa powder mixed with 1 ½ cups warm water
- 4 ½ cups water

Method:

1. Add rice and water in a saucepan. Place the saucepan over medium heat.
2. Let it boil for 15 minutes. Stir frequently.
3. Add cocoa mixture and stir constantly until well combined.
4. Add brown sugar and stir until it dissolves completely and the porridge is thick in consistency.
5. Serve in bowls. Drizzle some condensed milk on top and serve immediately.

Breakfast T-bone steak with Fried Eggs

Serves: 4

Ingredients:

- 2 T-bone steak (12 ounces each)
- ¼ teaspoon pepper powder (optional)
- 4 tablespoons olive oil
- 4 fried eggs
- 2 teaspoons salt
- 10 tablespoons butter
- 6 cloves garlic, smashed

Method:

1. Sprinkle salt over the steak and rub it well into it. Let it sit for 15 minutes.
2. Place a large pan over medium heat. Add butter. When butter melts, add oil, garlic and steak. Cook for 4-5 minutes. Flip sides and cook the other side for 3 minutes.
3. Remove butter-oil mixture with a spoon and drizzle over the steak.
4. Serve garnished with pepper if using and fried eggs.

Tortang Talong (Eggplant Omelet)

Serves: 4

Ingredients:

- 8 Asian eggplants
- Salt to taste
- Pepper to taste
- 4 large eggs, beaten
- Oil, to fry, as required

Method:

1. Place the eggplants in a broiler or on a grill and grill until blisters are formed on the skin. Remove from the grill and set aside to cool.
2. Peel the eggplants but do not discard the stem and crown.
3. Make the eggplants slightly flat with a fork but be careful not to break the eggplants.
4. Add eggs, salt and pepper into a bowl and whisk well.
5. Place a pan over medium high heat. Add some oil. When the oil is heated, dip the eggplant in the egg and place in the pan.
6. Repeat the above step with the remaining eggplants. Fry until golden brown on all the sides. Remove with a slotted spoon and place on a plate lined with paper towels.
7. Serve with rice of your choice and some sauce to accompany.

Vegan Tapa

Serves: 6

Ingredients:

- 2 cups dried, unseasoned non-gmo soy fillets or chunks
- 4 tablespoons vinegar
- 2 cups water
- 6 cloves garlic, peeled, crushed, minced
- ½ cup soy sauce
- 1 teaspoon pepper
- 2 tablespoons melted refined coconut oil or extra-virgin olive oil or more if required

Method:

1. Add soy fillets, vinegar, water, soy sauce and pepper into a pot. Place the pot over low heat. Cook for 30-40 minutes. Stir 2-3 times while it is cooking. Remove the fillets with a slotted spoon and place on a plate. When cool enough to handle, squeeze of excess moisture. Dry with paper towels. Set aside.
2. Place a pan over medium heat. Add oil. When the oil is heated, add garlic and cook until golden brown. Place the fillets in the pan. Cook until they turn a couple of shades darker and firmer to feel.
3. Serve hot with garlic fried rice or vinegar dip.

Tuyo with Rice and Tomato

Serves: 6

Ingredients:

- 24 tuyo salted dried fish
- 6 plum tomatoes, cut into wedges
- 1 cup spiced vinegar sinamak
- 6 cups cooked white rice
- Cooking spray

Method:

1. Take a large sheet of foil. Spray fish on either side with cooking spray and place on the foil. Cover with another sheet of foil and seal it well. Make a hole in the foil for the steam to escape.
2. Bake in a preheated oven at 400° F for about 6-10 minutes.
3. Place 4 pieces of fish in each plate. Add a cup of rice in each plate and place tomato wedges.
4. Drizzle spiced vinegar and serve.

Arroz Caldo

Serves: 3

Ingredients:

- ¾ pound chicken, cut into pieces
- 2 cups water
- ½ teaspoon garlic, minced
- ¾ cup rice, rinsed
- 1 tablespoon fish sauce
- ¼ teaspoon pepper
- 3 hardboiled eggs, peeled
- 1 knob ginger, julienned
- ½ chicken bouillon cube
- 1 tablespoon oil
- ½ cup onion, minced
- ½ cup green onions, minced
- 1 ½ tablespoons safflower kasubha
- Lemon wedges to serve
-

Method:

1. Place a pot over medium heat. Add oil. When the oil is heated, add onion, garlic and ginger and sauté until onions are translucent.
2. Add pepper and chicken cube and stir for a minute
3. Add chicken and cook until golden brown on all the sides.
4. Stir in the fish sauce and rice and sauté for 3-4 minutes.
5. Add water and stir. When it begins to boil, lower the heat and cover with a lid. Cook until rice is tender.
6. Add safflower kasubha and stir.
7. Add eggs and stir lightly.
8. Serve chicken and rice with egg, garlic, green onion and lemon wedges in each plate.

Lugaw, Tokwa't Baboy

Serves: 4

Ingredients:

- 3 cups rice
- ½ cup ginger, julienned
- Salt to taste
- Pepper to taste
- 2 cups fried tokwa (tofu)
- 2 quarts water
- 2 cloves garlic, minced, toasted
- 6 stalks spring onions
- Fish sauce to taste
- 2 cups baboy (pork ear strips)
- 2 tablespoons vegetable oil
-

Method:

1. Place a saucepan over medium heat. Add oil. When the oil is heated, add ginger and sauté until light brown. Add rice, fish sauce, pepper and salt and sauté for 3-4 minutes.
2. Add water and stir constantly until well combined. Cover with a lid and simmer until rice is soft and the porridge is thick in constituency.
3. Ladle into bowls.
4. Top with tokwa, spring onion, baboy and garlic. Sprinkle some pepper on top and serve.

Taho

Serves: 8

Ingredients:

For sago pearls:

- ½ cup sago pearls
- 12 cups water
- ½ cup dark brown sugar

For arnibal (brown sugar syrup):

- 1 cup dark brown sugar
- 1 cup water
- 1 teaspoon vanilla
- 2 pounds silken tofu
-

Method:

1. Add water and sugar into a large saucepan. Place the saucepan over high heat.
2. When it begins to boil, stir in the sago pearls. When it begins to boil again, lower the heat and cover with a lid. Cook until sago pearls are nearly translucent and a dot in the center of the pearls.
3. Drain the water and rinse in cold water. Drain and set aside.
4. To make arnibal: Add sugar, water and vanilla into a saucepan. Place a saucepan over medium heat. Stir constantly until the sugar dissolves completely. Turn off the heat.
5. Place tofu in a steamer and steam the tofu for 15 minutes.

6. Place equal quantity of tofu in 8 bowls. Divide the sago pearls and place over the bowls. Drizzle arnibal on top and stir.
7. Serve warm.

Pandesal

Serves: 16-20

Ingredients:

- 4 cups bread flour
- 4 cups all-purpose flour
- 1 cup white sugar
- 2 teaspoons baking powder
- 2 pouches rapid rise yeast
- 2 cups bread crumbs
- 2 tablespoons cooking oil
- 10 tablespoons butter, melted
- 2 ½ cups fresh, warm milk
- 2 teaspoons salt
- 2 eggs
-

Method:

1. Add milk, yeast and sugar into a bowl and stir until completely dissolved.
2. Add flour, salt and baking powder into a large mixing bowl and stir.
3. Pour the yeast mixture into the bowl. Also add butter, eggs and oil and mix with your hand until smooth dough is formed. Place in the bowl
4. Dust your countertop with a little flour. Place the dough on your countertop and knead until pliable. You can also knead using a stand mixer with dough attachment.
5. Cover the bowl with a moist cloth. Set aside in a warm place for a couple of hours.
6. Divide the dough into 4-5 parts and roll each part into a log. Slice on the diagonal into 4 to 5 parts each. In all you will be left with 16-20 slices.

7. Dredge in breadcrumbs and place on a baking sheet that is lined with parchment paper. Leave enough space between the rolls for it to rise. Let it stay on the baking tray for 15 minutes.
8. Bake in a preheated oven at 375° F for about 15 minutes.
9. Remove from the oven and cool for a few minutes.
10. Serve hot with coffee.

Note: These rolls are also served at any other meal.

Crispy Spamsilog

Serves: 4

Ingredients:

- 2 cans Spam meat, cut into bite size pieces
- 1 cup cornstarch
- ½ teaspoon garlic powder
- 4 eggs
- ¼ cup all-purpose flour
- Vegetable oil, as required

Method:

1. Whisk together eggs and garlic powder in a bowl.
2. Add flour and cornstarch into a shallow bowl and stir.
3. First, dip meat pieces in beaten eggs. Shake to drop off excess egg. Next coat in the flour mixture.
4. Coat once more in the flour mixture. Place on a plate.
5. Meanwhile, place a deep pan with oil (at least 2 inches from the bottom of the pan).
6. Drop 3-4 pieces of meat in the pan at a time and fry until brown and crisp on all the sides.
7. Remove with a slotted spoon and place on a plate lined with paper towels.
8. Repeat steps 6-7 with the remaining pieces of meat.
9. Serve with ketchup as a dip.

Tofu Arroz Caldo

Serves: 3

- ¾ pound fresh tofu, cut into pieces
- 3 ½ cups water
- ½ teaspoon garlic, minced
- ½ cup rice, rinsed
- 1 tablespoon fish sauce
- ¼ teaspoon pepper
- ½ inch ginger, thinly sliced
- ½ tablespoon vegetable oil + extra to deep fry
- ½ cup onion, minced
- 1 cup green onions, minced
- Lemon juice, to drizzle

Method:

1. Place a small deep pan over medium heat. Add oil so that it covers at least 2 inches from the bottom of the pan. When the pan is well heated, add tofu and fry until golden brown. Remove with a slotted spoon and place over a plate lined with paper towels.
2. Place a pan over medium heat. Add oil. When the oil is heated, add garlic and cook until golden brown. Add onion and ginger and sauté until onions are translucent.
3. Stir in the fish sauce and rice and sauté for 3-4 minutes.
4. Add water, salt and pepper and stir. When it begins to boil, lower the heat and cover with a lid. Cook until rice is tender and the mixture is creamy.
5. Add tofu and stir. Taste and adjust the seasonings if required.
6. If the porridge is too thick, dilute with a little water and heat thoroughly.
7. Add half the green onions and stir. Simmer for 5 minutes.

8. Ladle into bowls. Garnish with remaining green onions.
9. Drizzle some lemon juice on top and serve.

Chapter Two: Filipino Lunch Recipes

Bistek Wrap

Serves: 8

Ingredients:

- Juice of 10 calamansi's
- 1 teaspoon pepper
- 2 1/4 pounds sirloin, thinly sliced
- Romaine lettuce leaves, as required
- 2 large white onions, sliced
- 4 tablespoons brown sugar
- ½ cup soy sauce
- 4 tablespoons vegetable oil
- 8 medium flour tortillas

Method:

1. Add calamansi juice, pepper, brown sugar and soy sauce into a bowl and stir until the sugar dissolves completely.
2. Place the sirloin in it. Toss until the strips are well coated. Set aside for an hour to marinate.
3. Place a large skillet over medium heat. Add sirloin along with the marinating liquid. Let it simmer for 5 minutes. Turn off the heat.
4. To make the wraps: Place tortillas on your countertop. Place 1-2 lettuces leaves over each tortilla. Place some sirloin strips. Place onion slices on top.
5. Wrap the tortilla in the shape of a cone.
6. Serve.

BBQ Chicken Wrap

Serves: 4

Ingredients:

- 4 chicken breast halves (4 ounces each)
- 1 teaspoon vegetable oil
- 1 cup sharp cheddar cheese
- 2 teaspoons sea salt
- 1 cup BBQ sauce
- 4 large flour tortillas
- 12 cup purple cabbage, chopped
- 4 cups romaine lettuce, chopped
- ½ cup carrots, julienned
- 1 ½ cups green cabbage

Method:

1. Sprinkle salt over the chicken. Let it sit for 10 minutes.
2. Brush the chicken with oil.
3. Grill on a preheated grill for 3 minutes. Baste with BBQ sauce and grill for 3-4 minutes on each side.
4. When done, place on your cutting board. When cool enough to handle, cut into strips, crosswise. Brush with remaining BBQ sauce.
5. Place the tortillas on your countertop. Divide the vegetables equally among the tortillas. Sprinkle cheese on it followed by chicken slices.
6. Wrap like a burrito and serve.

Sinabawang Corned Beef

Serves: 6

Ingredients:

- 2 cans (11.5 ounces each) corned beef
- 2 large potatoes, peeled, cubed
- 4 cups water
- 6 tablespoons cooking oil
- 2 large yellow onions
- ½ cup parsley, chopped
- 4 cloves garlic, crushed, minced
- Salt to taste
- Pepper to taste

Method:

1. Place a pan over medium heat. Add oil. When the oil is heated, add onion and garlic and sauté until translucent.
2. Stir in the corned beef and cook for a couple of minutes.
3. Add potatoes and saute for 3-4 minutes. Add water and stir.
4. Lower the heat and cook until the potatoes are tender.
5. Add half the parsley. Add more water if desired. Add salt and pepper and stir.
6. Garnish with parsley and serve.

Bistek Silog

Serves: 8

Ingredients:

For Bistek Tagalog:

- 2 pounds beef sirloin, thinly sliced
- Juice of 2 lemons or 6 calamansi
- 6 cloves garlic, crushed
- 6 tablespoons oil
- ½ cup soy sauce
- 1 teaspoon pepper
- 2 large onions, cut into rings
- Salt to taste

To serve:

- 8 fried eggs
- 8 cups garlic fried rice

Method:

1. Add soy sauce, pepper and lemon juice into a bowl and stir. Add beef and toss well. Set aside to marinate for a couple of hours.
2. Place a skillet over medium heat. Add oil. When the oil is heated, add onion and sauté until translucent. Once done and set-aside on a plate.
3. Place the pan back over medium heat. Add the beef into the pan but retain the marinade.
4. Cook until beef is brown. Remove beef with a slotted spoon and set aside.
5. Add garlic into the pan and cook until light brown. Add the retained marinade.

6. When it begins to boil, add the beef back into the pan. Simmer until the beef is cooked through. Pour some water if required.
7. Add the onions and salt and mix well.
8. Serve hot with fried eggs and garlic-fried rice.

Chopsuey with Quail Eggs

Serves: 4

Ingredients:

- 31/4 ounces pork shoulder, thinly sliced
- ½ cup carrot slices, cut crosswise
- 1 small head cauliflower, cut into florets
- ½ cup red bell pepper, chopped
- ½ cup green bell pepper, chopped
- 1/3 small cabbage, cut into large pieces
- 8 quail eggs, boiled
- 3 cloves garlic, crushed, chopped
- 1 ½ tablespoons oyster sauce
- ¾ cup water
- Salt to taste
- Pepper to taste
- 1 shrimp cube
- 2 teaspoons cornstarch mixed with 2-3 tablespoons water
- 2 ½ tablespoons cooking oil

Method:

1. Place a pan over medium heat. Add oil. When the oil is heated, add onion and garlic and sauté until translucent.
2. Add pork and cook until light brown. Add oyster sauce and cook for 2-3 minutes.
3. Add shrimp cube and water and stir until well combined. When it begins to boil, cover with a lid and boil until water reduces to half its original quantity.
4. Add cauliflower and carrot and mix well.

5. Add cabbage, green bell pepper and red bell pepper and sauté for 3-4 minutes until the vegetables are crisp as well as tender.
6. Add cornstarch mixture and stir constantly until thick.
7. Add quail eggs and stir. Turn off the heat.
8. Serve.

Sinigang Na Hipon (Shrimps in Sour Soup)

Serves: 8

Ingredients:

- 3 pounds shrimp with head
- 2 cups string beans (sitaw), cut into 2 inch pieces
- 2 large white onions, quartered
- 2 packets sinigang mix tamarind soup base mix (1.4 ounces each)
- 6 tablespoons fish sauce
- 2 bunches water spinach (kangkong), cut into 3 inch pieces
- 4 medium tomatoes, quartered
- 16 cups water
- 4 banana peppers or long green peppers

Method:

1. Place a large cooking pot over medium heat. Add water. When it begins to boil, add tomatoes and onions and saute until translucent.
2. Stir in the sinigang mix and continue simmering.
3. Add string beans and banana pepper and cook for 3 minutes.
4. Stir in the fish sauce and shrimp and cook for 5 minutes. Finally, add water spinach and stir.
5. Remove from heat and cover with a lid. Let it rest for 5 minutes.
6. Serve with hot rice.

Misua

Serves: 8

Ingredients:

- 4 1/4 ounces misua
- 1 cup shrimp
- 2 cups cabbage, chopped
- 2 large red onions, minced
- 1 tablespoon oil
- Freshly ground pepper to taste
- 2 gourds or luffa or patola, sliced (optional)
- 1 cup pork belly, cubed
- 12 squid balls, quartered
- 8 cloves garlic, minced
- 4 cups chicken broth
- 1-2 teaspoons fish sauce or to taste

Method:

1. Place a large soup pot over medium heat. Add oil. When the oil is heated, add onion and garlic and saute until translucent.
2. Add pork belly and cook until brown and crisp. Add squid balls and cook until done.
3. Pour broth and add patola. When it begins to boil, let it cook for 4-5 minutes.
4. Add misua, cabbage and shrimp and simmer for 2-3 minutes.
5. Add fish sauce and pepper and mix well.
6. Serve hot.

Chicken Tinola

Serves: 8

Ingredients:

- 2 tablespoons oil
- 4 cloves garlic, minced
- 2 tablespoons fish sauce
- 4 cans (14 ounces each) chicken broth
- Salt to taste
- Pepper to taste
- 1 pound spinach, chopped
- 2 onions, chopped
- 3 inch fresh ginger, peeled, thinly sliced
- 6 pounds chicken legs and thighs, rinsed, pat dried
- 2 chayote squash, peeled, cut into bite size pieces
- 2 heads Bok Choy, chopped

Method:

1. Place a large pot over medium heat. Add oil. When the oil is heated, add onion and garlic and sauté until onions are translucent.
2. Add ginger and fish sauce and sauté for 4-5 minutes. Add broth and stir. Simmer for a few minutes.
3. Stir in the chayote and cook until the chicken is cooked through. Add Bok Choy, spinach, salt and pepper. Cook for a couple of minutes until the spinach wilts.
4. Ladle into bowls and serve.

Lumpia

Makes: 30

Ingredients:

- 4 tablespoons vegetable oil
- 6 cloves garlic, minced
- 2 cups carrots, shredded
- ½ cup water chestnuts, finely chopped
- 2 cups onion, finely chopped
- 2 pounds lean ground pork
- 1 cup green onions, thinly sliced
- 4-6 tablespoons tamari sauce
- 30 dried rice paper wrappers
- Pepper to taste
- 4 cups lukewarm water
- Salt to taste
- Sweet chili dipping sauce to serve

Method:

1. To make filling: Place a large pan over medium heat. Add oil. When the oil is heated, add onion and garlic and sauté until translucent.
2. Add pork, ½ cup green onion, carrots, soy sauce and water chestnuts and sauté until pork is cooked. Stir occasionally.
3. Turn off the heat and add into a large bowl. Add remaining green onions. Season with salt and pepper. Toss well.
4. Take one rice wrapper and dip in the bowl of lukewarm water. Let it remain dipped for a few seconds until it turns soft. Remove from the water and place on a moist kitchen towel.

5. Spread 2 tablespoons of the filling on 1/3 of the wrapper (the part that is closest to you). Fold inwards either of the sides and start wrapping tightly. Moisten the edges with water and press the edges to seal. Place with its seam side facing down. Place them next to each other. Do not pile them.
6. Repeat steps 4-5 and make the remaining.
7. Serve with sweet chili dipping sauce.

Lumpia can also be served as an appetizer or as a side dish.

Pako

Serves: 8

Ingredients:

- 8 pako leaves, rinsed, pat dried
- 2 red onions, sliced
- 4 tomatoes, sliced
- 2 salted eggs, sliced

For dressing:

- 4 tablespoons vinegar
- ½ teaspoon pepper powder
- ½ teaspoon salt
- 1 teaspoon sugar

Method:

1. To make dressing: Add all the ingredients of dressing into a bowl and whisk well. Set aside for a while for the flavors to set in.
2. Add pako, onion and tomato into a bowl and toss well.
3. Pour dressing on top and toss. Divide into plates. Place egg slices on top and serve.

Chicken Afritada

Serves: 12

Ingredients:

- 1 cup vegetable oil
- 2 tablespoon fresh ginger, chopped
- 1 cup soy sauce
- 4 teaspoons garlic salt
- 2 red bell peppers, cut into strips
- Pepper to taste
- 2 onions, chopped
- 2 whole chickens, cut into pieces
- 1 cup oyster sauce
- 2 cans (10 ounces each) tomato sauce
- 2 cans (10 ounces baby peas), drained
- 8 medium potatoes, peeled, cubed

Method:

1. Place a large skillet over medium high heat. Add oil. When the oil is heated, add ginger and onion and saute until light brown.
2. Place chicken with the skin side facing down. Cook until golden brown. Flip sides and cook until golden brown.
3. Add all the sauces and garlic salt into a bowl and whisk well. Pour over the chicken.
4. Add peas, potatoes and bell peppers and stir lightly. Cook until chicken is tender. Sprinkle pepper on top and serve with hot rice.

Pangat Na Isda (Pinangat or Pakisw)

Serves: 8

Ingredients:

- 2 inches ginger, sliced
- Pepper to taste
- 8 sapsap or talakitok fish
- 2 tomatoes, sliced
- 4 cloves garlic, minced
- 2 onions, sliced
- 2 green chilies, sliced
- 16 kamias, sliced
- Water, as required
- 5-6 tablespoons fish sauce + extra to serve

Method:

1. Place fish in a pan. Layer with the entire vegetables one over the other (each layer should have one type of vegetables).
2. Spread fish sauce on top. Pour about ½ cup water on top.
3. Cover with a lid. Place the pan over medium heat. Cook for 15 minutes.
4. Serve with hot rice and some more fish sauce.

Tokneneng (Filipino Street Food)

Serves: 3

Ingredients:

- 6 eggs, hardboiled, peeled
- 2 tablespoons cornstarch or more if needed
- Vegetable oil for deep frying

For sauce:

- 2 tablespoons ketchup
- 2 tablespoons rice vinegar
- 1 teaspoon soy sauce
- 2 tablespoons brown sugar

For batter:

- ½ cup all-purpose flour
- Few drops red and yellow food coloring
- Salt to taste
- Pepper to taste
- ¼ cup water

Method:

1. To make sauce: Add rice vinegar, soy sauce, brown sugar and ketchup into a small saucepan. Place the saucepan over medium heat. Stir until sugar dissolves completely. Turn off the heat and cool completely.
2. To make batter: Add flour, red coloring, yellow coloring, salt, pepper and water into a bowl and whisk well. Adjust the coloring to get a deep orange color.
3. Place a deep pan over medium heat. Pour enough oil so cover at least 3 inches from the bottom of the pan. Let the

oil heat. It should heat well but not smoking. When the eggs have to be added, the temperature of the oil should be 375° F.

4. Dredge the eggs in cornstarch. Shake to drop off excess cornstarch. Dip into the batter. Insert a bamboo skewer and carefully lower it into the oil. Fry until the outer covering is crisp on all the sides. Add 2 to 3 eggs in a batch.

5. Remove with a slotted spoon and place on a plate lined with paper towels.

6. Repeat steps 4-5 and fry the remaining eggs.

Quick and Easy Pancit

Serves: 3

Ingredients:

- 2 packages (12 ounces each) dried rice noodles
- 2 onions, finely chopped
- 4 cups cooked chicken breast meat, diced
- 8 carrots, thinly sliced
- Lemon wedges to garnish
- 2 teaspoons vegetable oil
- 6 cloves garlic, minced
- 1 large head cabbage, thinly sliced
- ½ cup soy sauce

Method:

1. Add rice noodles into a large bowl. Pour enough warm water to cover the noodles. Let it soak in it for a while until it becomes soft. Drain and set aside the noodles.
2. Place a wok or large skillet over medium heat. Add oil. When the oil is heated, add onion and garlic and sauté until translucent.
3. Add chicken, carrot and cabbage and stir well. Add soy sauce and stir again. Sauté until the cabbage is slightly tender.
4. Add noodles and toss well. Heat thoroughly. Stir constantly after adding the noodles.
5. Serve garnished with lemon wedges.

Chapter Three: Filipino Dinner Recipes

Soups and Stews:

La Paz Batchoy (Filipino Pork Noodle Soup with Shrimp Paste)

Serves: 3

Ingredients:

- 6 tablespoons vegetable oil
- ½ tablespoon sugar
- 1 small onion, sliced
- 1 ½ tablespoons kosher salt
- 1 scallion, thinly sliced, to garnish
- ½ tablespoon shrimp paste
- 2 cloves garlic, minced
- 4 cloves garlic, thinly sliced
- 1 pound pork butt
- ½ pound miki noodles
- Pork cracklings, to garnish

Method:

1. Place a saucepan over medium high heat. Add ½ tablespoon oil. When the oil is heated, add shrimp paste, minced garlic, sugar and onions and sauté for 3-4 minutes.
2. Stir in the pork, salt and 3-½ cups water. Bring to a boil.
3. Lower the heat and cover with a lid. Simmer until pork is tender. It can take couple of hours.
4. Remove pork with a slotted spoon and place on your cutting board. When cool enough to handle, slice the pork.

5. Pass the broth in the saucepan through a strainer placed over a bowl. Discard the solids and pour the broth back into the saucepan.
6. Add noodles into the saucepan. Boil for 5 minutes.
7. Meanwhile, place a pan over medium heat. Add ½ tablespoon oil. When the oil is heated, add sliced garlic and sauté until golden brown.
8. Remove garlic with a slotted spoon and place on a plate lined with paper towels.
9. Ladle soup with noodles into bowls. Place pork slices in each bowl.
10. Sprinkle garlic slices, pork cracklings and scallions on top and serve.

Pancit Molo

Serves: 10—12

Ingredients:

For wontons:

- 1 pound shrimp, chopped
- 1 pound shrimp, chopped
- 1 large eggs
- 2 packages wonton wrappers
- Salt to taste
- Freshly ground pepper to taste
- 2 teaspoons sesame oil
- 2 tablespoons cornstarch
- 2-3 tablespoons chopped chives
- Salt to taste
- 2 teaspoons sesame oil

For Molo soup:

- 2 chicken breasts, boiled, flaked
- 2 bunches spring onions, chopped
- 2 small onions, minced
- 8 cloves garlic, thinly sliced, fried – follow step 7-8 in the previous recipe
- Sesame oil, to drizzle
- 12 cups chicken broth
- 8 cloves garlic, minced
- Fish sauce to taste
- Leftover wonton wrappers
- Pepper to taste

Method:

1. To make wontons: Add all the ingredients for wontons except wonton wrappers into a bowl and stir.
2. Place some filling on the center of the wonton wrappers. Fold to shape into wontons. Press the edges to seal. Set aside on a plate.
3. To make molo soup: Place a soup pot over medium heat. Add oil. When the oil is heated, add onion and garlic and saute for a few minutes until translucent.
4. Add chicken and saute for 3-4 minutes.
5. Add broth and bring to the boil. Drop the wontons in the boiling broth. Let it boil for 3 minutes. Add leftover wonton wrappers and boil for a couple of minutes.
6. Add fish sauce and pepper and stir.
7. Ladle into soup bowls. Sprinkle spring onions and fried garlic. Drizzle some sesame oil on top and serve.

Lomi

Serves: 12

Ingredients:

- 2 1/4 pounds lomi or any other thick egg noodles
- 20 squid balls, halved
- ½ head cabbage, shredded
- 12 cups chicken stock
- 6 eggs, beaten
- 2 shallots, finely chopped
- Pepper to taste
- 3 cups pork belly, cubed
- 24 medium prawns
- 2 large carrots, julienned
- 4 tablespoons cornstarch
- 12 cloves garlic, minced
- 1 tablespoon vegetable oil
- Fish sauce to taste

Method:

1. Cook the noodles following the instructions on the package. Set aside.
2. Place a soup pot over medium heat. Add oil. When the oil is heated, add pork belly and cook until golden brown. Remove pork with a slotted spoon and set aside.
3. Add shallots and garlic into the pot and cook for a minute.
4. Add squid balls and cook for a couple of minutes.
5. Pour stock and stir. When it begins to boil, add prawn and pork and boil for a couple of minutes.
6. Whisk cornstarch in a little water and add into the pot. Stir constantly until thick.

7. Add the cooked noodles, cabbage and carrots and let it boil again.
8. Add pepper and stir. Turn off the heat.
9. Stirring continuously, add the eggs.
10. Add fish sauce to taste.
11. Ladle into soup bowls and serve.

Savory Mussels

Serves: 8

Ingredients:

- 4 tablespoons olive oil
- 4 cloves garlic, minced
- 2 stalks celery, sliced
- 4 ½ pounds mussels, cleaned, de-bearded
- 2 onions, chopped
- 2 carrots, sliced
- 6 ½ cups chicken broth
- 2 bunches fresh spinach, rinsed, torn in half

Method:

1. Place a soup pot over medium heat. Add oil. When the oil is heated, add onion and garlic and saute until translucent.
2. Add carrot and celery and cook until slightly tender.
3. Add broth and allow it to boil for 5 minutes.
4. Drop the mussels into the pot and cover with a lid. Cook until they start opening. Discard the ones that do not open.
5. Add spinach and turn off the heat.
6. Ladle into soup bowls and serve.

Sopa de maiz

Serves: 2

Ingredients:

- 1 ½ cups onions, thinly sliced
- 1 pound raw shrimp, shelled, deveined, diced
- 4 cups water
- 3 cups cooked or canned corn
- 4 cloves garlic, minced
- 4 cups bottled clam juice
- 1 teaspoon freshly ground pepper
- 1 cup watercress or spinach, shredded
- 1 tablespoon oil

Method:

1. Place a soup pot over medium heat. Add oil. When the oil is heated, add onion and garlic and sauté for a few minutes until translucent.
2. Stir in the shrimp. After 2 minutes, add water, clam juice, corn and pepper.
3. When it begins to boil, lower the heat and simmer for 10-12 minutes.
4. Add watercress and simmer for 2 minutes.

Nilaga (Filipino Chicken Stew)

Serves: 8

Ingredients:

- 16 chicken drumsticks
- ¼ cup fresh ginger, peeled, thinly sliced
- 3 tablespoons soy sauce
- 4 celery ribs, sliced
- 4 russet potatoes, peeled, cut into 1 inch cubes
- 2 Napa cabbages, sliced
- 8 cups water
- 1 teaspoon peppercorns
- 2 onions sliced
- 2 small carrots, peeled, sliced
- 2 tablespoons olive oil

Method:

1. Place a pot with chicken, water, peppercorns, celery, carrot, ginger, onion and soy sauce over high heat.
2. Do not cover and let it boil about 25-30 minutes.
3. Meanwhile, place a pan over high heat. Add oil. When the oil is heated, add potatoes and cook until brown.
4. Add potatoes and cabbage and stir. Lower the heat to low heat and cook for 10 minutes.
5. Cook until potatoes are tender.
6. Ladle into bowls and serve.

Ensaladang Pinoy (Filipino Vegetable Salad)

Serves: 4

Ingredients:

- 2/3 cup white vinegar
- 2 teaspoons fish sauce
- ½ - 2/3 cup sugar
- 4 cucumbers, thinly sliced
- 3-4 red onions, thinly sliced
- 1 inch ginger, peeled, thinly sliced
- 4 green chilies, sliced
- 3-4 red bell peppers, cut into strips
- 8 cloves garlic, crushed
- 6 stalks lemongrass, white part only, pounded lightly

Method:

1. To make picking solution. Add vinegar, 2/3-cup water and sugar. Place the saucepan over medium heat. Stir until sugar dissolves completely. Turn off the heat and cool completely.
2. Add fish sauce and stir.
3. Toss together rest of the ingredients. Transfer into a large jar with a lid. Use 2 smaller jars if you do not have a larger jar.
4. Add pickling solution. The solution should cover all the vegetables. Fasten the lid and refrigerate for a minimum of 24 hours. It can last for 2-3 days.
5. Serve as it is or add some lettuce leaves and tomatoes if desired, just before serving. Toss well and serve.

Filipino Mango and Tomato Salad

Makes: 4-6 cups

Ingredients:

- 2 large firm, ripe mangoes, peeled, julienned
- 1 small red onion, chopped
- 2 large Roma tomatoes, deseeded, chopped
- 1 bunch cilantro, leaves only, chopped
- 6 tablespoons fish sauce
- 2 tablespoons sugar
- ½ cup vinegar
- 2 teaspoons canola oil
- ½ teaspoon freshly ground pepper

Method:

1. Add mangoes, onion, tomatoes and cilantro into a large bowl and toss.
2. Add rest of the ingredients into a small bowl and whisk well until sugar dissolves completely. Pour over the salad. Toss well.
3. Cover the bowl and chill for 15-20 minutes.
4. Toss again and serve.

Bok Choy in Oyster Sauce

Serves: 4

Ingredients:

- 2 bundles Bok Choy leaves, halved lengthwise
- 2 tablespoons sesame oil
- 1 teaspoon cornstarch
- 4 tablespoons canola oil
- 4 tablespoons soy sauce
- 6 cloves garlic, minced
- 5-6 tablespoons oyster sauce
- 6 tablespoons water

Method:

1. Steam, the Bok Choy, leaves and rinse in cold water. Drain and set aside.
2. Place a wok over medium heat. Add canola oil. When the oil is heated, add garlic and sauté until light brown.
3. Remove garlic with a slotted spoon and set aside.
4. Whisk together in a bowl, soy sauce, oyster sauce, water and cornstarch and pour into the wok. Stir constantly until thick.
5. Add half the garlic back into the wok. Add Bok Choy and stir.
6. Mix well.
7. Serve Bok Choy topped with sauce. Drizzle sesame oil on top and sprinkle remaining garlic.
8. Serve.

Shrimp Fried Rice

Serves: 8

Ingredients:

- 6 eggs, whisked
- 2 tablespoons olive oil
- 2 tablespoons soy sauce
- 4 cloves garlic, peeled, minced
- 1 medium onion, finely chopped
- 1 pound medium sized shrimp, shells and head intact
- 6 tablespoons butter
- 4 tablespoons oyster sauce
- 6 green onions, chopped
- 2 carrot, diced
- 8 cups cooked rice, chilled
- 2 cup frozen peas, thawed

Method:

1. Place a wok over medium heat. Add oil. When the oil is heated, add egg and stir until the eggs are cooked as per your liking. Transfer into a bowl and set aside.
2. Place the wok over heat. Add 2 tablespoons butter. When butter melts, add shrimp and cook until pink on either side. Remove with a slotted spoon and place in the bowl of eggs.
3. Add remaining butter into the wok. When it melts, add onions and sauté until soft.
4. Add rice and both the sauces. Sauté for a few minutes until heated thoroughly.
5. Add carrots and peas and cook until carrots and peas are tender.
6. Add shrimp and eggs back into the wok and mix well.

7. Add green onions and cook for a couple of minutes until it wilts. Season with salt and pepper.
8. Serve.

Filipino Camote Cue (Caramelized Sweet Potatoes on a Stick)

Serves: 20

Ingredients:

- 2 pounds sweet potatoes, peeled, cut into ½ inch slices
- 2- 2 ½ cups vegetable oil, for frying
- 2 cups brown sugar

Method:

1. Place a deep pan with oil over medium heat. When the oil heats, add 1-cup sugar. In a while, the sugar will melt and float on top of the oil.
2. Add half the sweet potatoes and cook for a few minutes. Sprinkle ¼ cup sugar over the sweet potatoes and fry until golden brown. Remove with a slotted spoon and place on a plate lined with paper towels.
3. Repeat the previous step and fry the remaining sweet potatoes.
4. Thread the sweet potato pieces on to bamboo sticks.
5. Serve hot.

Eggplant Adobo

Serves: 8-10

Ingredients:

- 10 cups eggplant, diced into 1 ½ inch cubes
- 4 tablespoons vegetable oil
- ½ cup red wine vinegar
- Freshly ground pepper to taste
- A pinch salt (optional)
- 2/3 cup soy sauce
- 12 cloves garlic, minced

Method:

1. Place eggplant cubes on layers of paper towels. Season with salt. Let it remain on the paper towels for 30 minutes. Dry the eggplants by patting with some more paper towels.
2. Place a saucepan with vinegar, pepper, soy sauce and garlic over medium heat. Boil for 5 minutes.
3. Stir in the eggplant and cover with a lid. Lower the heat and simmer for 7-8 minutes. Stir a couple of times while it is cooking.
4. Serve.

Filipino Monggo Beans and Pechay (Mung Beans and Bok Choy)

Serves: 8

Ingredients:

- 4 cups green mung beans, cooked
- 5-6 medium tomatoes, chopped
- 2 onions, chopped
- 3 cups Bok Choy, chopped
- Salt or soy sauce to taste
- 2 tablespoons ginger, minced
- 4 cloves garlic, minced
- 2 cups vegetable broth

Method:

1. Add onion and a little broth into a blender and blend until smooth. Add ginger while blending if desired or else let it remain minced.
2. Pour into a large pan Add ginger, garlic and tomatoes and simmer for 4-5 minutes.
3. Add mung beans and broth and bring to a boil. Add Bok Choy and cook for 5-8 minutes.
4. Add salt or soy sauce and stir.
5. Serve over hot rice.

Meat, Poultry, Seafood and Vegetarian Main Course:

Adobo Chicken Wings

Serves: 3-4

Ingredients:

- 1 pound whole chicken wings, tips removed, drummets and flats separated
- 6 tablespoons soy sauce
- 4 cloves garlic, crushed
- ¼ cup mayonnaise
- A handful fresh cilantro, minced
- ¼ teaspoon ground ginger
- ¼ teaspoon garlic powder
- Zest of ½ lime, finely grated
- ¼ teaspoon ancho chili powder
- 6 -7 tablespoons rice vinegar
- ¼ teaspoon whole black peppercorns
- 1 bay leaf
- ¼ cup sour cream
- Kosher salt to taste
- ½ tablespoon fresh lime juice
- ½ Fuji apple, cored, cut into ¼ inch thick slices

Method:

1. Add 6 tablespoons rice vinegar, crushed garlic, 2/3-cup water, peppercorns, bay leaf and soy sauce into a bowl and stir. Add chicken wings and toss well.
2. Cover with cling wrap and chill for 30 minutes.
3. Add chicken along with the marinade into a Dutch oven. When it begins to boil, cover with the lid and place pot in the oven.
4. Bake in a preheated oven at 400° F for about 30 minutes.

5. Take out the pot from the oven and transfer on to a baking sheet that is lined with foil. Retain about 2 tablespoons of the cooked liquid and throw off the remaining.

6. Set the oven on to the broiler setting. Place the baking sheet in the oven and broil for 8-10 minutes. Flip halfway through broiling. Broil until crisp.

7. Add 1-tablespoon rice vinegar, sour cream, ginger powder, garlic powder, salt, cilantro, mayonnaise and lime zest into a bowl and whisk well. Chill until use.

8. Add lime juice, chili powder, apple slices and a pinch of salt in a bowl and toss.

9. Serve hot chicken wings with mayonnaise mixture as dip and apple slices.

Filipino Barbecue Chicken Skewers

Serves: 3

Ingredients:

- 1 ¼ pounds chicken thighs, skinless, cut into 1 ½ inch pieces
- ¼ cup banana ketchup
- 2 tablespoons Sprite
- 3 cloves garlic, minced
- ½ tablespoon light brown sugar
- 1 tablespoon canola oil, to brush chicken while grilling
- Crispy garlic slices, to serve – refer the 1st recipe in this chapter
- ¼ cup soy sauce
- 1 tablespoon freshly ground pepper
- 1 ½ tablespoons fresh lemon juice
- ½ teaspoon fresh ginger, minced
- 1 teaspoon kosher salt
- Scallions, sliced, to garnish

Method:

1. Set aside the crispy garlic and scallions and rest of the ingredients into a bowl and toss well.
2. Cover the dish with plastic wrap and place in the refrigerator overnight.
3. Insert the chicken on to skewers. Do not discard the marinade.
4. Brush the chicken with oil. Grill on a preheated grill. Baste with the marinade and grill until cooked. It should take around 12 minutes.
5. Place grilled chicken on a serving platter. Sprinkle crispy garlic and scallions and serve.

Filipino Chicken Adobo

Serves: 3-4

Ingredients:

- 2-2 ½ pounds chicken thighs
- ¼ cup soy sauce
- ½ teaspoon black peppercorns
- ¼ cup white vinegar
- 2 cloves garlic, crushed
- Steamed rice, to serve

Method:

1. Add all the ingredients except rice into a bowl and toss well.
2. Place the bowl in the refrigerator for 2-3 hours.
3. Transfer into a skillet. Place the skillet over high heat. When the mixture begins to boil, lower the heat and cover with a lid. Simmer for 20-30 minutes. Stir a couple of times while it is cooking.
4. Uncover and simmer until sauce is thickened and the chicken cooked through.
5. Serve over hot steamed rice.

Spinach Laing

Serves: 5-6

Ingredients:

- 2 pounds spinach, shredded
- 2-3 cups coconut milk
- 2 tablespoons garlic, minced
- 5-6 tablespoons Bagoong (shrimp paste
- 1 tablespoon vegetable oil, or more if required
- 1 pound pork, diced or thinly sliced
- 2 onions, minced
- 2 inch piece ginger, thinly sliced
- 4 red chili peppers, chopped

Method:

1. Place a wok over high heat. Add oil. When the oil is heated, add garlic and onions and sauté until translucent.
2. Add ginger and sauté until aromatic.
3. Stir in the pork and lower the heat to medium heat. Cook for 5 minutes.
4. Stir in the shrimp paste and chilies and mix well.
5. Add 2 cups coconut milk. When it begins to boil, add spinach and stir.
6. Lower the heat to low heat and cover with a lid. Simmer until nearly dry. Stir a couple of times while it is cooking.
7. Serve over hot steamed rice.

Pork and Shrimp Pancit

Serves: 8

Ingredients:

- 2 packages (6.75 ounces each) rice noodles
- 2 small onions, minced
- 1 teaspoon ground ginger
- 3 cups cooked pork, chopped
- 6 tablespoons oyster sauce
- ½ teaspoon crushed red pepper flakes
- 10 tablespoons vegetable oil, divided
- 4 cloves garlic, minced
- 3 cups cooked small shrimp, diced
- 8 cups Bok Choy, shredded
- ½ cup chicken broth
- 2 green onions, minced

Method:

1. Add warm water into a large bowl. Add rice noodles and let it soak for 20 minutes. Drain the water and set aside.
2. Place a large wok over medium high heat. Add 6 tablespoons oil. When the oil is heated, add noodles and cook for a couple of minutes.
3. Remove the noodles and place in a bowl. Keep it warm.
4. Add 4 tablespoons oil into the wok. When the oil is heated, add onion, ginger, garlic, pork and shrimp and sauté for a minute.
5. Add Bok Choy, chicken broth, red pepper flakes and oyster sauce and stir.
6. Cover with a lid and cook until Bok Choy wilts.
7. Divide the noodles into individual serving plates. Serve the pork mixture over the noodles.
8. Sprinkle green onion on top and serve.

Lechon Kawali (Crispy Pan-Fried Roasted Pork)

Serves: 4-8

Ingredients:

For crispy pork:

- 3 pounds pork liempo (pork belly), chopped into bite size pieces
- 4 bay leaves
- Salt to taste
- Oil, for frying
- 6 cloves garlic, crushed
- 2 teaspoons peppercorns or pepper powder
- Water, as required

For sauce:

- 6 tablespoons soy sauce
- 2 shallots or 2 small onions, minced
- 2 chili peppers, chopped (optional)
- 10 tablespoons vinegar
- 2 cloves garlic, minced

Method:

1. To make crispy pork: Add all the ingredients except oil into a pan. Cover with water.
2. Place the pan over medium heat. When it begins to boil, lower the heat and cook until the skin is soft.
3. Drain the water and cool completely. Let it dry for a while in the open air.
4. Place a small deep pan over medium heat. When the oil is well heated but not smoking, add some pork pieces and

cook until golden brown and a few bubbles appear on the skin.

5. Meanwhile, make the sauce by mixing together all the ingredients.

Bellychon (Crispy, Slow Roasted Pork Belly)

Serves: 3-4

Ingredients:

- ½ cup + ½ tablespoon sugar
- ¼ cup + 1 tablespoon kosher salt
- 8-9 cloves garlic, smashed
- 2 pounds pork belly, boneless, butterflied
- ¼ cup coconut vinegar
- 1 stalk lemongrass
- 2 tablespoons canola oil
- ½ cup white vinegar
- 1 tablespoon + ¼ teaspoon whole black peppercorns
- 2 bay leaves
- 2 shallots, peeled
- 1 whole star anise
- 1 small whole Thai red chili
- 1/8 cup cilantro roots + leaves to garnish
- 4 cups water

Method:

1. To make brine: Add ½ cup sugar, ¼ cup salt, white vinegar, 2 cloves garlic, star anise, ½ tablespoon peppercorns, bay leaves and water into a saucepan.
2. Place the saucepan over high heat. Stir constantly until sugar and salt dissolves.
3. Turn off the heat and cool completely.
4. Add pork and stir until pork is well coated with the mixture.
5. Place in the refrigerator for 7-8 hours.
6. To make dipping sauce: Add ½ tablespoon sugar, ½ tablespoon salt, white vinegar, 2 -3 garlic cloves, ½

tablespoon peppercorns chili and coconut vinegar into a blender and blend until smooth.

7. Transfer into a bowl and cover with a lid. Chill until use.
8. Add garlic, shallot, remaining salt, lemongrass, cilantro roots and remaining peppercorns into the food processor bowl. Blend until smooth and well combined.
9. Take out the pork from the brine and rub this paste inside the belly. Roll it and fasten with a string.
10. Place in a roasting pan.
11. Bake in a preheated oven at 275° F for about 3-4 hours or until cooked through.
12. Cool completely and let it dry in the open air for 7-8 hours.
13. Place a skillet over medium high heat. Add oil. When the oil is heated, place pork belly and cook until crisp and golden brown on all the sides.
14. Remove pork and place on your cutting board. When cool enough to handle, cut the pork into thin slices of ¼ inch thickness, crosswise.
15. Serve pork slices with dipping sauce.

Biocol Express

Serves: 4-6

Ingredients:

- 2 1/4pounds pork, sliced or chopped into small pieces
- 8 cloves garlic, crushed
- 2 onions, sliced
- 4 cups coconut milk
- Salt to taste
- Pepper to taste
- 5-6 tablespoons bagoong (shrimp paste)
- 10-12 finger chilies, sliced
- 4 tablespoons cooking oil
- 20 beans (Baguio beans)

Method:

1. Place a pan over medium heat. Add oil. When the oil is heated, add onion and garlic and sauté until golden brown,
2. Add meat and cook until brown.
3. Stir in the shrimp paste and finger chilies.
4. Stir in the coconut milk, salt, pepper and Baguio beans. Cook until meat is tender and the sauce has thickened.
5. Serve hot.

Beef Caldereta

Serves: 3-4

Ingredients:

- 1 pound beef, cubed
- 1 small onion, chopped
- ½ cup bell pepper, cut into strips
- 1 medium carrot, sliced
- 1 small clove garlic, crushed
- ¼ cup tomato paste
- ½ cup tomato sauce
- ½ cup cheese, grated
- ½ tablespoon Tabasco sauce (optional)
- 3 small potatoes, sliced
- Salt to taste
- Pepper to taste
- 1 ½ -2 cups water
- 1/3 cup liver, spread
- ½ cup pineapple juice, unsweetened
- 2 bay leaves

Method:

1. Add water and beef into a saucepan. Place the saucepan over medium heat. Bring to the boil. Cook until the meat is tender.
2. Stir in the pineapple juice and onion and lower the heat. Let it simmer.
3. Place a small pan over medium heat. Add garlic and a few drops of oil and cook until light brown. Add the garlic clove into the simmering beef mixture.
4. Stir in the liver spread, tomato sauce and tomato paste and continue simmering for 10 minutes.

5. Stir in the bay leaves, carrot, bell pepper and potatoes. Cook until the vegetables are tender.
6. Add salt, pepper, cheese and Tabasco sauce if using and stir. Cook until cheese melts.
7. Discard the bay leaves. Add some water if you find the gravy very thick.
8. Serve over hot cooked rice.

Filipino Beef Steak

Serves: 3-4

Ingredients:

- 2 pounds New York strip steak, thinly sliced
- Juice of ½ lemon
- ½ teaspoon white sugar
- ½ tablespoon cornstarch
- 1 ½ tablespoons olive oil
- 1 clove garlic, chopped
- 1 ½ tablespoons soy sauce
- Salt to taste
- Pepper to taste
- 2 tablespoons vegetable oil
- 1 clove garlic, chopped

Method:

1. Add soy sauce, lemon juice, salt, pepper and sugar into a bowl and whisk well.
2. Add steak into the bowl and toss until well coated. Sprinkle cornstarch over the steak and toss lightly.
3. Cover the bowl with plastic wrap and chill for 1-8 hours.
4. Place a skillet over medium heat. Add vegetable oil. When the oil is heated, add beef slices without the marinade (shake to drop off excess marinade from the steak strips).
5. Place beef slices in the pan and cook for 2-4 minutes on each side or until they begin to get firm.
6. Remove beef with a slotted spoon and set aside on a plate.

7. Place a small skillet over medium heat. Add olive oil. When the oil is heated, add onion and garlic and cook until golden brown.
8. Spread over the beef slices.
9. Serve.

Filipino Beef Stir-Fry

Serves: 2

Ingredients:

- 1 ¼ pounds New York strips steaks, sliced into thin strips
- 1 tablespoon soy sauce
- 1 ½ tablespoons olive oil
- 1 clove garlic, crushed
- Salt to taste
- Pepper to taste
- 1/3 cup green peas
- 1 stalk celery, sliced
- 2 tablespoons oil
- 1 tablespoon cornstarch
- ¾ teaspoon white sugar
- 1 small onion, chopped
- ½ tablespoon oyster sauce
- ½ pound snow peas
- 1 small carrot, sliced
- ½ red bell pepper, deseeded, cut into 1 inch squares

Method:

1. Add soy sauce, lemon juice, salt, pepper and sugar into a bowl and whisk well.
2. Add steak into the bowl and toss until well coated. Sprinkle cornstarch over the steak and toss lightly.
3. Cover the bowl with plastic wrap and chill for 2-8 hours.
4. Place a skillet over medium heat. Add olive oil. When the oil is heated, add onion and garlic and cook until translucent.
5. Add oyster sauce, green peas, snow peas, celery, carrot, bell pepper, salt and pepper. Stir-fry for a few minutes

until the vegetables are tender as well as crisp. Turn off the heat.

6. Place a skillet over medium heat. Add vegetable oil. When the oil is heated, add beef slices without the marinade (shake to drop off excess marinade from the steak strips).

7. Cook for 2-4 minutes on each side or until they begin to get firm.

8. Remove beef with a slotted spoon and add into the pan of vegetables and mix well. Heat thoroughly.

Goat Caldereta

Serves: 2

Ingredients:

- 1 pound goat meat, cut into 1 ½ inch cubes
- ¾ teaspoon salt or to taste
- 3 cloves garlic, peeled, minced
- 1 inch cinnamon sticks
- 2 teaspoons tomato paste
- Freshly ground pepper to taste
- 1 small red bell pepper, cut into ¼ inch strips
- 1 ½ tablespoons white vinegar
- 2 tablespoons olive oil
- 1 medium onion, peeled, minced
- 1 bay leaf
- 1 medium potato, chopped into 1 inch cubes
- ½ tablespoon whole black peppercorns
- 1 cup water

Method:

1. Add vinegar, salt, pepper and meat into a bowl and toss well. Let it marinate for 40-45 minutes.
2. Place a strainer over a bowl. Add meat into the strainer. Set aside the liquid. Dry the meat by patting with paper towels.
3. Place a heavy saucepan over medium heat. Add oil. When the oil is heated, add meat in a single layer. Cook until brown on all the sides.
4. Remove meat with a slotted spoon and place on a plate.
5. Add onion and garlic into the pan and sauté for a couple of minutes.

6. Add cinnamon, peppercorns and bay leaf. Sauté for a minute.
7. Add meat back in into the saucepan along with the released juices, retained marinade, water and tomato paste.
8. Lower the heat. Cover with a lid and cook for 10 minutes.
9. Add potatoes and stir. Cover and cook until meat and potatoes are tender.
10. Add bell pepper and cook for 3-4 minutes.
11. Serve over hot steamed rice.

Kalderetang Kambing

Serves: 4

Ingredients:

- 2 pounds goat meat, cubed
- 2 large carrots, sliced
- 2 medium onions, minced
- 1 ½ cups green peas
- 2 cups tomato sauce
- 2 medium potatoes, quartered
- 4 cloves garlic, minced
- 1 ½ cups red bell pepper, sliced
- 6 medium tomatoes, diced
- 12 tablespoons liver spread
- 1 teaspoon crushed chili flakes
- 4 cups water
- 12 tablespoons liver spread
- Salt to taste
- Pepper to taste
- 2 tablespoons cooking oil

Method:

1. Sprinkle salt generously over the meat and set aside for an hour.
2. Rinse well. Scrape off the salt from the meat.
3. Place a wok over medium high heat. Add oil. When the oil is heated, add garlic and onions and sauté until translucent.
4. Add tomatoes and cook until the tomatoes are slightly soft.
5. Add meat and cook until light brown.

6. Stir in the crushed chili, tomato sauce and liver spread. Let it cook for 3-4 minutes.
7. Add water and stir. Cook until meat is tender.
8. Add potatoes, peas and carrots and cook until tender. Add bell pepper and stir. Cook for a couple of minutes until crisp as well as tender.
9. Add more water if you find the gravy very thick. Add salt and pepper and stir.
10. Serve over hot steamed rice.

Ginataang Langka (Jackfruit in Coconut Milk)

Serves: 8

Ingredients:

- 2 pounds unripe langka (Jackfruit), deseeded, sliced
- 2 onions, chopped
- 3-4 inches fresh ginger, peeled, sliced and crushed
- 4 tablespoons bagoong alamang (shrimp paste) optional
- 1 cup water
- 1 pound shrimp
- 8 cloves garlic, crushed first and then peeled
- 6 cups coconut milk
- 4 green or red chili peppers, slit
- Salt to taste
- 2 tablespoons cooking oil

Method:

1. Place a large pan over medium heat. Add oil. When the oil is heated, add garlic and cook until golden brown. Add ginger and sauté for 8-10 seconds.
2. Add onions and sauté until translucent.
3. Stirring constantly, add the coconut milk. Keep stirring until it boils.
4. Add shrimp paste, jackfruit and chilies. Sauté for a couple of minutes.
5. Add water and stir. Cook until tender.
6. Stir in the shrimp and simmer until shrimp is cooked.
7. Serve over steamed rice.

Spicy Ginataang Hipon

Serves: 8

Ingredients:

- ¾ pound medium shrimp with head and shells
- 6 long green peppers siling pansigang, thinly sliced
- 4 tablespoons ginger, minced
- 1 cup scallions, chopped
- ½ teaspoon pepper
- Fish sauce to taste (optional)
- 2 packs Knorr Ginataang Gulay mix
- 4-10 pieces bird's egy chili siling labuyo, chopped (depending on how hot you prefer)
- 2 medium onions, sliced
- 8 cloves garlic, crushed
- 1 ½ cups lukewarm water
- 6 tablespoon cooking oil

Method:

1. Whisk together Ginataang Gulay mix and lukewarm water in a bowl and set aside. This is called gata.
2. Place a pot over medium heat. Add oil. When the oil is heated, add onion, ginger and garlic and sauté until onions are translucent.
3. Add green peppers, chili and scallions and sauté for a minute.
4. Add gata and stir. When it begins to boil, add shrimp and cook for 5 minutes.
5. Add pepper and fish sauce and mix well. Let it boil for a couple of minutes.
6. Serve in bowls along with rice.

Adobong Pusit (Squid Adobo)

Serves: 10

Ingredients:

- 4 ½ pounds squid, cleaned
- 1 cup water
- 4 tablespoons olive oil
- 4 cloves garlic, minced
- 2 tablespoons soy sauce
- 1 cup white vinegar
- Salt to taste
- Pepper to taste
- 2 small onions, minced
- 2 tomatoes, chopped

Method:

1. Add water, vinegar, salt, pepper and squid into a pot. Place the pot over medium heat. When it begins to boil, let it simmer for 10 minutes.
2. Meanwhile, place a saucepan over medium heat. Add oil. When the oil is heated, add onion and garlic and sauté until onions are translucent.
3. Add tomatoes and soy sauce and stir. Add the squid along with the cooked liquid and stir. Let it simmer for 20 minutes.

Clams in Oyster Sauce

Serves: 8

Ingredients:

- 2 onions, chopped
- 4 inches fresh ginger, peeled, grated
- 4 tablespoons olive oil
- 4 ½ pounds clams in shells
- 4 cloves garlic, minced
- 4 tablespoons oyster sauce
- 1 cup water

Method:

1. Place a wok over medium heat. Add oil. When the oil is heated, add onion and garlic and sauté until translucent.
2. Add ginger and sauté for a minute until fragrant.
3. Whisk in oyster sauce. Cover and cook for 2 minutes.
4. Add water and cover again. Simmer for 2 minutes.
5. Add clams and cover again. In 4-5 minutes most of the clams should open. Throw off the clams that do not open.
6. Serve.

Fried Crablets

Serves: 8

Ingredients:

- 4 1/2 pounds crablets
- 2 tablespoons oil
- Salt to taste
- Magic Sarap seasoning to taste
- Pepper to taste
- Vinegar to dip

Method:

1. Place a large frying pan over medium heat. Fry the crabs in batches.
2. Add about a tablespoon of oil. Add some crabs and season with salt. Cook until orange in color.
3. Season with magic sarap and pepper.
4. Transfer on to a serving platter.
5. Dip in vinegar while eating.

Filipino Vegetarian Pancit Bihon

Serves: 6-8

Ingredients:

- 2 packages (16 ounces each) rice noodles
- 1 bunch Bok Choy or pechay, chopped, keep the stems separate
- 10-12 cloves garlic, chopped
- 1 large onion, chopped
- 4 green onions, sliced
- 2 cups vegetable stock or water or more if required
- Lemon slices to serve
- 2 inches ginger, peeled
- 4 carrots, julienned
- Soy sauce, to taste
- 2-3 tablespoons coconut oil

Method:

1. Soften the rice noodles following the instructions on the package and set aside.
2. Place a wok over medium heat. Add oil. When the oil is heated, add garlic and ginger and sauté for a minute.
3. Add mushroom and Bok Choy stalks into the wok. Pour vegetable broth and soy sauce.
4. When the water begins to boil, add Bok Choy leaves and carrots. Add rice noodles and lower the heat. Stir until well combined. If there is no broth left in the wok, then add some more broth.
5. Add some more soy sauce and stir.
6. Serve hot.

Adobong Gulay

Serves: 8

Ingredients:

- 2 onions, chopped
- ½ teaspoon whole peppercorns or to taste
- 4-5 tablespoons vegetable oil
- ½ cup soy sauce
- Pepper to taste
- ½ teaspoon sugar
- 6 cloves garlic, sliced
- 4 bay leaves
- 2 pounds potatoes or eggplants, cubed
- ½ cup sukang paombong or vinegar of your choice
- 8 hardboiled eggs (optional)

Method:

1. Place a pan over medium high heat. Add oil. When the oil is heated, add peppercorns and bay leaves.
2. Add garlic after 2-3 seconds. Cook until brown. Add onions and sauté until soft.
3. Stir in the pepper and sugar and sauté for a few seconds.
4. Add vinegar and soy sauce and mix well.
5. Lower the heat to medium heat. Add potatoes or eggplants and stir-fry for a couple of minutes.
6. Lower the heat and cook until soft. It should not be overcooked. Add a sprinkle water if it is too dry while it is cooking.
7. Prick the eggs lightly with a fork and add into the pan when the potatoes are nearly cooked.
8. Serve with rice.

Vegetarian Lugaw

Serves: 4-5

Ingredients:

- 1 ½ tablespoons canola oil or vegetable oil, divided
- ½ tablespoon garlic, sliced
- ¼ cup wood ear mushrooms
- ½ cup sweet rice, rinsed
- ½ cup jasmine rice, rinsed
- 1 small onion, chopped
- ½ tablespoon ginger, minced
- 6 cups water, divided
- Salt to taste
- A large pinch paprika
- ½ teaspoon soy sauce

For sautéed mushrooms:

- 2 shiitake mushrooms
- Salt to taste
- ½ teaspoon sesame oil
- ½ teaspoon olive oil
- ½ teaspoon paprika
- 2 eggs (optional)

Method:

1. Place wood ear mushrooms in a bowl of hot water for a few minutes until soft.
2. Drain and place on your chopping board. Cut into smaller pieces.
3. Place a heavy saucepan over medium heat. Add oil. When the oil is heated, add a pinch of salt, ginger, garlic and onions and sauté until onions are soft.

4. Add both the rice and sauté for a minute. Add water, salt, paprika and stir.
5. Raise the heat to high heat. When it begins to boil, lower the heat and simmer for 20 minutes. Add water while simmering if required.
6. Meanwhile, make sautéed mushrooms as follows: Chop the shiitake mushroom and shred the stem of the mushrooms using your fingers.
7. Add the mushroom (pieces as well as the shredded) into a bowl. Add sesame oil and olive oil and toss.
8. Sprinkle paprika and salt and toss well. Massage the mushrooms with your fingers for a couple of minutes.
9. Place a pan over medium heat. Spray the pan with cooking spray. Add mushrooms and sauté until tender.
10. Ladle the porridge into bowls. Top with sautéed mushrooms and serve.

Pansit Grisado (Stir Fried Rice Noodles)

Serves: 3-4

Ingredients:

- 2 tablespoons vegetable oil
- 2 ounces Spanish onions, julienned
- 1 clove garlic, peeled, minced
- ½ pound tofu, pressed of excess moisture, cut into 1 ½ inch strips
- 2 tablespoons soy sauce
- ¼ ounce fish sauce
- 2 ounces celery, julienned
- 4 ounces vegetarian sausages, cut into strips of 1 ½ inches
- Salt to taste
- Freshly ground pepper to taste
- Lemon wedges to serve
- 2 tablespoons cornstarch
- 1 pint vegetable broth
- 7 ounces carrots, cut into julienne strips
- 7 cabbage leaves, thinly sliced
- ½ pound rice noodles, soaked in warm water until soft, drained
- 2 scallions, chopped, to garnish

Method:

1. Place a wok over medium high heat. Add oil. When the oil is heated, add garlic and onions and sauté until onions are soft.
2. Add tofu and stir. Cook until brown.
3. Stir in the broth, soy sauce, carrot, fish sauce, celery, vegetarian sausage and cabbage and stir.

4. Lower the heat and cook until the vegetables are crisp as well as tender.
5. Add noodles and stir. Raise the heat to medium low and heat thoroughly.
6. Add salt and pepper and stir.
7. Garnish with scallions and serve with lemon wedges.

Gluten Guisado

Serves: 2-3

Ingredients:

- ¾ cup ground gluten
- ½ tablespoon garlic, minced
- ½ can sweet peas
- 1 small onion, sliced
- ½ tablespoon oil
- ¾ cup potatoes, cubed
- 1 small tomato, thinly sliced
- Salt to taste
- Pepper to taste
- 2 tablespoons raisins
- ¼ cup water

Method:

1. Place a skillet over medium heat. Add oil. When the oil is heated, add onion and tomatoes and cook until soft.
2. Stir in the ground gluten, salt and pepper and sauté for 5-6 minutes.
3. Add potatoes and water and stir. Cook until tender.
4. Add peas and raisins and stir. Turn off the heat.
5. Serve hot.

Chapter Four: Filipino Dessert Recipes

Cassava Cake

Serves: 20

Ingredients:

- 4 cups yucca, peeled, grated
- 2 cans (12 ounces each) evaporated milk
- 2 cans (14 ounces) coconut milk
- 4 eggs, beaten
- 2 cans (14 ounces each) sweetened condensed milk

Method:

1. Add all the ingredients into a mixing bowl and whisk until well combined.
2. Spoon into a greased baking dish lined with parchment paper.
3. Bake in a preheated oven at 350° F for about 60 minutes. Broil for 2-3 minutes or until top is brown. Cool completely.
4. Chill for a couple of hours. Slice and serve.

Maja Blanca (Coconut Pudding)

Serves: 5

Ingredients:

- ¼ cup water
- ½ cup coconut milk
- ¼ cup white sugar
- 2 tablespoons sweetened coconut flakes, toasted
- ¼ cup cornstarch, whisked with 3-4 tablespoons water
- 6 tablespoons water
- 2 tablespoons fresh sweet corn kernels
- A little butter to grease

Method:

1. Grease a baking dish with a little butter.
2. Add coconut milk, water and sugar into a saucepan. Place the saucepan over low heat. Stir until sugar dissolves completely.
3. When the mixture begins to boil. Stir in the corn and cornstarch mixture. Stir constantly until the mixture thickens.
4. Let it boil again. Continue simmering until smooth and well thickened.
5. Spoon into the baking dish. Cool for a few hours until firm.
6. Sprinkle toasted coconut flakes and serve.

Puto

Serves: 9

Ingredients:

- 2 cups all-purpose flour
- ½ tablespoon baking powder
- 6 ounces canned evaporated milk
- 1 cup + 2 tablespoons Edam cheese, shredded
- 1 cup white sugar
- 3 eggs
- ¾ cup water

Method:

1. Add flour, baking powder and sugar into a bowl and stir.
2. Whisk together in a bowl, eggs, evaporated milk and water. Add the flour mixture and whisk until well combined.
3. Pour into greased puto molds or ramekins. Sprinkle cheese on top.
4. Pour enough water to fill a saucepan (2 inches from the bottom of the saucepan). Place the saucepan over medium high heat. Place a steamer basket in it.
5. When the water begins to boil, place the molds on the steamer basket.
6. Cover and simmer for 30 minutes or a toothpick when inserted in the center comes out clean.
7. Place on the wire rack to cool.
8. Serve warm.

Taisan (Filipino Chiffon Cake)

Serves: 15-20

Ingredients:

- 2 ½ cups cake flour, sifted
- 1 teaspoon salt
- 1 teaspoon vanilla extract
- ½ cup evaporated milk
- 1 tablespoon unsalted butter, melted
- 2 teaspoons baking powder
- Yolks of 8 large eggs
- ½ cup sugar
- 3 tablespoons water
- ½ cup vegetable oil

For egg white side:

- Whites of 12 large eggs
- 1 cup sugar
- ½ teaspoon cream of tartar

For topping:

- Melted butter
- Sugar to sprinkle
- ½ cup white cheddar cheese, grated

Method:

1. Grease a large loaf pan with butter or use 2 smaller loaf pans.
2. Stir together cake flour, salt and baking powder in a bowl.
3. Add yolks, ½ cup sugar, butter, vanilla, milk, water and oil into a bowl and whisk well.

4. Add the flour mixture into the bowl of yolks and beat with an electric beater constantly for a couple of minutes until smooth.

5. Add cream of tartar and remaining sugar into the bowl of whites and set the beater on low speed. Beat for a minute.

6. Raise the speed to medium speed and beat until medium peaks are formed.

7. Pour into the batter. Fold gently and pour into the loaf pan or pans.

8. Bake in a preheated oven at 325° F for about 35-45 minutes or a toothpick, when inserted in the center, comes out clean.

9. Remove from the oven and cool for 10 minutes. Remove from the pan and place on a plate.

10. Brush butter on top of the cake. Sprinkle sugar first over the buttered cake and finally cheese.

11. Slice and serve.

Leche Flan with Cream Cheese

Serves: 24

Ingredients:

- 2 cups granulated sugar
- 8 ounces cream cheese, softened
- 2 cans (10.1 ounces each) sweetened condensed milk
- 10 large eggs
- 2 cans (12.5 ounces each) evaporated milk
- 2 teaspoons vanilla extract

Method:

1. Divide the sugar equally into 2 loaf pans. Place the loaf pans over medium heat. In a while, the sugar will dissolve and caramelize. Turn off the heat and cool for a few minutes. Shake the pans so that the caramel spread all over the bottom of the pan.
2. Add rest of the ingredients into a blender and blend until smooth. Divide the mixture into the 2 loaf pans.
3. Place the loaf pans in a larger baking pan. Pour enough water in the baking pan to cover the loaf pan up to half the height of the loaf pan (This is a water bath).
4. Bake in a preheated oven at 350° F for about 1 ½ hours or until set.
5. Remove from the water bath and cool completely. Chill for a few hours.
6. Run a knife around the edges of the flan to loosen.
7. Invert on to a plate. Cut into slices and serve.

Cornbread Bibingka

Serves: 20-25

Ingredients:

- 2 cups rice flour
- 1/8 teaspoon salt
- 6 eggs
- 6 tablespoons unsalted butter, melted
- 2 cans (14.5 ounces each) cream style corn
- 2 cups yellow cornmeal
- 2 tablespoons baking powder
- 2 cups sugar
- 2 cans (14.5 ounces each) coconut milk

For topping:

- Granulated sugar, as required
- Unsalted butter, melted, as required

Method:

1. Grease a large square baking dish with a little oil.
2. Add rice flour, salt, cornmeal, salt and baking powder into a bowl and stir.
3. Add eggs into another bowl and whisk until frothy. Add butter and sugar and whisk until frothy.
4. Add the rice flour mixture and coconut milk and whisk until well combined.
5. Mix in the creamed corn.
6. Spoon the batter into the baking pan.
7. Bake in a preheated oven at 350° F for about 35-45 minutes or a toothpick, when inserted in the center, comes out clean.

8. Remove from the oven and cool for 10 minutes. Remove from the pan and place on a plate.
9. Brush butter on top of the cornbread. Sprinkle sugar on top. Cut into squares and serve.

Kutsinta (Filipino Sticky Cake)

Serves: 24

Ingredients:

- ½ cup tapioca starch
- ½ cup brown sugar
- ½ teaspoon salt
- 2 2/3 cups water + extra for steaming
- 1 ½ cups all-purpose flour, sifted
- 1 cup sugar
- ½ teaspoon baking soda
- Grated coconut to serve

Method:

1. Add water (for steaming) into a large pan (fill up to half the height of the pan) and place over high heat.
2. Add tapioca starch, salt, flour and baking soda into a bowl and stir.
3. Pour 2 2/3 cups water into the mixture and whisk until well combined and free from lumps. If you are not able to get rid of the lumps, then pass the mixture through a strainer placed over a bowl.
4. Pour into 2 twelve-count muffin or 4 six-count tins (fill up to half) that are greased with butter.
5. Steam in batches. Add water in the pan while steaming each batch.
6. Place the muffin tin in the simmering water. Cover the pan with lid. Steam for 25-30 minutes.
7. Remove from the water and set aside the muffin tin. Cool for some time. Loosen the edges of Kutsinta with a knife. Cool completely.
8. Serve with grated coconut.

Mamon (Filipino Sponge Cake)

Serves: 24

Ingredients:

- 1 ¾ cups + 1 ½ tablespoons cake flour
- ½ teaspoon salt
- ½ cup water
- 1 teaspoon vanilla extract
- 3 teaspoons baking powder
- 8 egg yolks
- 2/3 cup granulated sugar
- 6 tablespoons vegetable oil

For meringue:

- 8 egg whites
- ½ cup granulated sugar
- ½ teaspoon cream of tartar

For topping: (Optional)

- Melted unsalted butter
- Granulated sugar to sprinkle
- ½ cup cheddar cheese, grated

Method:

1. Stir together cake flour, salt and baking powder in a bowl.
2. Add yolks, sugar, vanilla and water into a bowl and whisk well.
3. Add the flour mixture into the bowl of yolks and beat with an electric beater constantly for a couple of minutes until smooth.
4. Add oil and stir. Set aside until meringue is prepared.

5. To make meringue: Add whites and cream of tartar in a mixing bowl. Beat with an electric mixer on high speed until foamy and airy.
6. Add sugar and beat until medium peaks are formed. Add meringue into the batter and cold gently, add a little at a time and fold each time.
7. Pour into 2 twelve-count muffin tins that are greased with butter or place baking cups in the muffin cups. Fill up to 2/3.
8. Place rack in the center of the oven.
9. Bake in a preheated oven at 325° F for about 15-18 minutes or a toothpick, when inserted in the center, comes out clean.
10. Remove from the oven and cool for 15 minutes.
11. Run a knife around the edges of the cakes to loosen.
12. Invert on to a plate.
13. Brush butter on top of the cakes. Sprinkle sugar first over the buttered cakes and finally cheese.
14. Serve.

Filipino Ube (Purple Yam) Halaya Ice Cream

Serves: 10

Ingredients:

- 4 cups ube halaya
- 4 cups heavy cream
- 4 teaspoons vanilla extract
- 2 cup macapuno or young coconut flesh, cut into strings
- 4 cups fresh whole milk
- 2 cups sweetened condensed milk

Method:

1. Set aside macapuno and add rest of the ingredients into a mixing bowl. Blend until smooth.
2. Pour into a bowl and chill for 3-4 hours.
3. Transfer into an ice cream maker and churn the ice cream following the manufacturer's instructions.
4. When the ice cream attains soft serve consistency, add macapuno and continue churning until the ice cream is ready.
5. Alternately, after step 2, pour into an airtight freezer safe container and freeze until firm.
6. Scoop and serve.

Gulaman Fruit Salad

Serves: 12

Ingredients:

- 2 bars red gulamam (gelatin)
- 2 cans (14.75 ounces each) fruit cocktail
- 4 cups boiling water
- 2 cans (7.6 ounces each) Nestle thick cream

Method:

1. Add gulaman in boiling water and stir until it dissolves completely. Transfer into a large Pyrex dish.
2. Add fruit cocktail with its juice and cream and stir. Chill until set.
3. Cut into small squares and serve.

Conclusion

I want to thank you once again for purchasing this book.

A typical Filipino meal consists of rice that is served with different sides. Filipino cuisine is vibrant and lively, quite similar to the inhabitants of this region.

With the help of recipes in this book, you will be able to dish out gourmet Filipino food within no time. Now, all that you need to do is gather all the necessary ingredients and start cooking. Select a recipe that strikes your fancy and experiment a little in the kitchen. The next time you have guests over for a meal, you can wow them with a traditional Filipino meal that will certainly win them over. Once you understand the basic flavors and combinations of ingredients, you can experiment with different ingredients and come up with new recipes.

Thank you and all the best.

Other Books by Grizzly Publishing

"Jamaican Cookbook: Traditional Jamaican Recipes Made Easy"

https://www.amazon.com/dp/B07B68KL8D

"Brazilian Instant Pot Cookbook: Delicious Pressure Cooked Meals Made Fast and Easy"

https://www.amazon.com/dp/B078XBYP89

"Norwegian Cookbook: Traditional Scandinavian Recipes Made Easy"

https://www.amazon.com/dp/B079M2W223

"Casserole Cookbook: Delicious Casserole Recipes From Around The World"

https://www.amazon.com/dp/B07B6GV61Q

Made in the USA
Las Vegas, NV
08 February 2022

43507765R00069